MIND
GAMES

MIND
GAMES

Sandra Woodcock

Published in association with
The Basic Skills Agency

Hodder & Stoughton

A MEMBER OF THE HODDER HEADLINE GROUP

Acknowledgements
Cover: Angelo Cavalli, Image Bank/Getty Images

Orders: please contact Bookpoint Ltd, 130 Milton Park, Abingdon, Oxon OX14 4SB. Telephone: (44) 01235 827720, Fax: (44) 01235 400454. Lines are open from 9.00–6.00, Monday to Saturday, with a 24 hour message answering service.

British Library Cataloguing in Publication Data

Woodcock, Sandra
  Mindgames. – (Chillers) (Livewire)
  1. Readers – English fiction
  I. Title   II. Basic Skills Agency
  428.6

ISBN 0 340 86951 8

First published 1997
This edition published 2002
Impression number   10 9 8 7 6 5 4 3 2 1
Year   2006 2005 2004 2003 2002

Typeset by Fakenham Photosetting Ltd, Fakenham, Norfolk.
Printed in Great Britain for Hodder & Stoughton Educational, a division of Hodder Headline Plc, 338 Euston Road, London NW1 3BH by Athenaeum Press Ltd, Gateshead, Tyne & Wear.

Contents

1

All Alone

Sam looked at the notice.
He wanted to go on the trip.
He had never been to Alton Towers,
but he didn't want to go by himself.
It was OK for the other students.
They all had girlfriends or boyfriends.
Ann was going with Dave.

DAY TRIP
Alton
Towers
23 July

2

Liz was going with Paul.

But Sam didn't have a girlfriend.

He didn't want to go by himself.

It would spoil the trip.

'Come on, Sam' said Mike.

'Put your name down. We need to fill the bus.'

In the end Sam put his name down.

The trip was the last day of term.

On the bus Sam sat by himself.

He looked out of the window.

He listened to his Walkman.

Liz and Paul tried to talk to him.

But he didn't say much.

After that no-one bothered him.

Sam looked at Liz.

She had her arm round Paul.

'I wish I had a girlfriend,' Sam thought.

They arrived at Alton Towers.
Sam wished he had not come.
Alton Towers was great fun.
But only if you were with friends.
Would he like it on his own?
'Come round with us Sam,' said Dave.
'Come with us if you like,' said Liz.
'We don't mind.'
But Sam thought she did mind.
She wanted to be with Paul.
Just the two of them.
'I'm OK,' said Sam. 'I'll see you later.'

He went to buy some chocolate.
He had a walk round.

He looked at other people.

They were enjoying themselves.

Sam had a camera with him.

He took some photos.

He was standing by the Big Wheel.

Someone tapped him on the shoulder.

It was a girl.

'Excuse me,' she said.

'I just dropped my earring.

I think you are standing on it.'

2
Sarah

_____

Sam looked down on the ground.
There was a small gold earring.
He picked it up.
'Are you by yourself?' the girl asked.
Sam looked surprised. 'Yes, I am.'
'Well, I am too,' she said.
'Would you go on that ride with me?'

She pointed at the Big Wheel.
'I don't want to go on by myself.
I'm scared.'

Sam didn't need asking twice.
'Put my earring in your pocket,' she said.
'I might lose it again.'
They went on the Big Wheel.
Then the Roller Coaster,
and the Haunted House.
They went on the water ride.
They got soaking wet.

'Let's get a pizza,' said Sam.
They ate pizza and drank hot chocolate.
Soon they were warm and dry again.
The girl said her name was Sarah.

She was very pretty.
She had pale skin and long fair hair.
She was quiet – like Sam.
He liked her a lot.
'Let me take a photo of you,' he said.
They were by the boating lake.

At first she wouldn't let him.
But then she smiled.
She said, 'Yes, all right, but be quick.'
He took lots of photos of her.
At four o'clock Sarah suddenly said,
'Oh Sam, I have to go now.'

3
Parting

_____

'Wait a minute!' said Sam.
'Tell me your other name!
What's your phone number?
Where do you live?'

Sarah walked away. Sam began to panic.
'Tell me your phone number,' she said.

Sam found a bit of paper.
He wrote down his number.
He gave it to Sarah.
'You will ring, won't you?' he begged.
Sarah smiled and waved.
Then she walked away.

Sam felt all mixed up.
He was so happy.
He felt he was floating on air.
But he felt sad too.
He had a sinking feeling inside.
He felt in a dream.
He nearly missed the bus.
They all cheered when he got on.
'Sam, at last we can go!
You're the last one.'

Sam said he was sorry.

He sat down by himself.

He looked out of the window.

He listened to his Walkman.

No-one asked about Sarah.

No-one had seen him with her.

At home Sam stayed up till midnight.

He was waiting for the phone to ring.

But it didn't ring.

He waited the next day.

And the next.

A week went by.

Sarah still had not phoned.

Sam felt very low.

He went into college.

He needed some books.

Liz and Ann were in the coffee bar.

'Hi, Sam!' they shouted.

'Come and look at our photos.'

4
Missing!

Sam sat down.

They had some photos of Alton Towers.

Sam thought of his own film.

It was still in the camera.

'Look at this one of Dave,' said Liz.

'He looks really silly.'

'I think you're on one, Sam,' said Liz.

'I took one of the water ride.
You were right at the front.'

Sam took the photo.
His eyes nearly popped out.
He was there on the ride
– but he was by himself!
The seat next to him was empty.
But Sarah had been next to him.
Why wasn't she in the photo?
Had Liz seen Sarah on the ride?
He didn't dare ask her.

'What's wrong?' asked Liz.
But Sam didn't say a word.
He dropped the photo.
He ran out of the coffee bar.

He ran all the way home.
Where was the camera?
He looked for it everywhere.
It took him half an hour.
He took out the film.
He ran to the shop.
'Could you do it in half an hour?' he asked.
'Come back in an hour,'
the girl in the shop said.

He went back in an hour.
The photos were ready.
He opened the packet.
His hands were shaking.
He looked at the photos quickly.
Sarah wasn't on any of them.
The photo of the boating lake was there.

The boats had come out well.
The fence was there.
Sarah had been standing near it.
But she wasn't in the photo.
It was the same with all the photos.
He had taken about ten of Sarah.
But she wasn't on any of them.
He couldn't believe it.

Sam thought back to that day.
He had asked a man to take a photo of them.
– Sam and Sarah together.
The photo was there.
But Sam was by himself.
There was no Sarah.
He couldn't believe it.

Was he going mad?
Had he really met Sarah?
Or was it all in the mind?
He walked home slowly.
He went to his room.
He threw the photos into a drawer.
He didn't look at them again.
He wanted to talk about Sarah.
But there was no-one to talk to.
No-one knew about her.

5
Hope

Weeks went by.

He kept thinking about Sarah.

He couldn't rest.

He couldn't think about anything else.

One morning his mum came into his room,

'I just washed your denim jacket,' she said.

'I found this.'

She held up a small gold earring.
Sam took it from her.
He held it tight.
He smiled and closed his eyes.
'Please come back, Sarah',
he said softly.